BACKLASH
PRESS

A pioneering publishing house dedicated to creating intelligent, vivid books.

Established to inform, educate, entertain and provoke.

Poetry Press

A Backlash Book
First published 2020
Reprinted 2024

ISBN: 978-1-91-62666-5-0

Backlash Press
71 Goldstone Crescent, Hove,
BN3 6LS, England
backlashpress.com
info@backlashpress.com

All rights reserved. No part of this publication may be reproduced, stored in a retrieval system or transmitted in any form or by any means, electronic, mechanical, photocopying, recording or otherwise, without permission of the copyright holder.

Copyright © Darren Demaree 2020

The moral rights of the author have been asserted.

Photographs (pages 36-41): Ryan Barker, Midwest Nostalgia, 1995-2020
Book & Cover Design: The Scrutineer, Rachael Adams
Fonts: Baskerville, Bree serif
Printed by IngramSpark

By the same author

Bombing the Thinker

Unfinished Murder Ballads

Darren Demaree

Contents

That Was Fairly Clear	/9
The Banker Took His Lunch to the Park	/10
The Assistant Manager of the Verizon Kiosk Holds His Cinnabon Soda for the Last Time	/11
The Inventor of Small Things Ends His Denial	/12
The Lawyer's Secretary Forgets Her Fifty Cents	/13
The Luminous Conjunction	/14
The Oldest Friends In Ohio Settle All of Their Old Grudges	/15
The Only Dedicated Cowboy in Columbus, Ohio Objects to the Price of his Black Coffee	/16
The Rain Storm Has Teeth	/17
The Sea Naked	/18
The Stuff of Legends	/19
The Walls Slid Back Down, Joining	/20
Through the Skin of the Lip	/21
We Gave Metal to Butterflies	/22
We Take More Photographs of the Dead Boy	/23
The Gym Shoe Dead	/24
A Flowering Almond	/25
The Facts Persisted	/26
The High School Baseball Coach Gets Exactly What He Wanted	/27
The Cage is Unwound by The Poetry of Death	/28
Somewhere Else You Will Have to Die	/29
Strobe-Effect	/30
Rubber Tied	/31
So Far From Lunar Air	/32
Sand Overspread	/33
Secret Thing	/34
Skyless	/35
Some Folks Inherit	/42

It Was A Question of Ownership	/43
Present and Turned Around	/44
Just A Twirling	/45
Leaning Into the Wind Doesn't Make You Part of the Wind	/46
Lilac Horses	/47
An Argument Erupts Over the Naming of Flowers	/48
She Made It No Further Than Nebraska	/49
In Some Towns There Is Only One Public Official and One Sex Worker	/50
It's Awful How Romantic This Is	/51
It Can't Be Reached and It Won't Go Away	/52
Kicking Horses	/53
I Can Tell By the Way You Talk	/54
The Woman Finds Her Ex-Lover in an Alley in Philadelphia	/55
Cut the Meat	/56
A Creamy Chiffon Dress	/57
Brazen Lake Superior	/58
Cockleshells	/59
Before She Put the Photograph to Her Chest She Flipped the Face Away from Her Flesh	/60
The Black Belly Star Dances Too	/61
Blank Light	/62
An Impression	/63
An Imperfect Comb	/64
A Misinterpretation of Big Love	/65
A Generous Sample of Enlightenment	/66
When the Swimmer Drowns	/67
The Girl Was A Raspberry	/68
Caribou	/69

That Was Fairly Clear

The flowers grew around the sketch of the bird that was pasted over the face of the boy that served as coal for the whole display. He paid for the minerals of each consciousness; he wanted to lose every layer of thought. He had post-burial goals, they all do, the artists that forget about the rain that comes with the storm. They embrace the thunder, they love that they are lightning, they always forget about what a real flood can do to a corpse that no one is willing to protect.

The Banker Took His Lunch to the Park

Suited, facing away from the brick wall, it was winter, yet no fist had arrived to confirm it, and when the banker sat down with his grocery store sandwich and iced tea, he saw no children running anywhere. They were in school, right? It was pleasant, this was a good idea he had, a sober lunch, away from his co-workers. Winter was coming and too soon the blowing sand from the play area would carry a deep cold with it. True, dark minds don't wait for the seasons to change. For them, it's always killing season, and when an excellent suit arrives alone, hangs itself to be inspected, the inspector must oblige. Selected to be shreds of a body, the banker never felt the flood overtaking him, he saw only the empty swings, waiting for a good leg kick.

The Assistant Manager of the Verizon Kiosk Holds His Cinnabon Soda For The Last Time

Always sipping life, he took gulps of the new girl at Cinnabon, cornered her at an apartment pool party his boss had thrown, and when everyone spilled out of the pool, they stayed in the shallow end, unable to come to any terms, he flipped to sign his final contract all over her first, red disappointment. Stolen from her father's pharmacy, she gave him a special, free drink from the deepest part of her heart. Enough of it spilled that the liquid found the escalator and it sparked a full hour before they found him, hands clinched around the best he could do.

The Inventor Of Small Things Ends His Denial

Not a creator of bones, but a creator of better marrow, he spent years on the door handle, but never understood the wood his creation could move. So, when his lock splintered through the doorframe, the thieves never appreciated the fact that they were pissing all of over the gentleness of a great artist. They took the blood from the un-bold. They implanted him with the grandness of death. They cornered him in the corner of his own world, and never even checked his palms to see what small tinker he was holding when the boot-print of the other side of the door came crashing in.

The Lawyer's Secretary Forgets Her Fifty Cents

That chipped State Highway Patrol dish, stained with ketchup and coffee, appearing to be gentle only to the change it collected for each pop the staff bought rang without coin all throughout the day, but when the building manager, who first earned that dish, did the daily count of off-brand refreshment, he felt the fire he used to feel pulling over a foreign car for being a foreign car, and as he marched into each office, looking for an empty can he found one on the desk of the lawyer's secretary, and that bitch, the one with two candy jars, that always had her kids hanging around coloring, hadn't even finished the damn drink. He could see her Toyota pulling out of the parking lot, and though he was going to lose the building soon, he needn't lose his respect for the way things worked around here. He took off slowly, the only way he could, hoping to catch her before she left his property.

The Luminous Conjunction

Black grass and the wilderness without a touch of water, without a bark of possibility, and the landscape then becomes as much of a monster as any animal that ever passed through it. Any slow walk through a land like that will turn a person into a pet, a product of the environment that surrounds like a hug, like a choke, like a fist, swallowed. Un-swaying, you will want to kick your legs, but that will only speed up your loss. Nature has never bothered with masks.

The Oldest Friends In Ohio Settle All Of Their Old Grudges

Cancer(ed), aided by the wind, their skin was free of every other love, and what was left for them had nothing left to give. Two old men that had told each other to go to hell a hundred times over seventy years, had meant it every time, and had apologized half of the time, shared a porch and hatched a plan to get drunk one last time, together, to get functionally insane, to have those minds make love to the cancer inside of them, and to erupt with the two pistols they were keeping at the bottom of the cooler. Both men got real drunk. Both men loaded a pistol. Both men knew of the infidelity, that one of the men had slept with the other's wife forty-five years ago, and it was that man that wanted one last pull of whiskey before they shot each other. He always did get what he wanted, he almost always got what he wanted.

The Only Dedicated Cowboy In Columbus, Ohio Objects To The Price Of His Black Coffee

Slenderness worn from where muscle once wanted to grow, then grew only to fit the active frame and casting of a man who had no room in his world for the modernity of the city he lived in, he knew that if he was going to have the energy to make it through his day as a chew-spitting communications technician at AT&T, he would need a lunch time coffee. Up at dawn, he had tended to his crop on the fire escape, he had fed all the animals before he fed himself, and all three of his cats appreciated that sort of man. Now, though, the slack before him was demanding two dollars for a black coffee, and that wore on him the way a bad hand would have worn on the Duke. His father had been a tax attorney, and bequeathed him no rifle. He would need to go to the pawn shop again.

The Rain Storm Has Teeth

Without a clink, a tink, or a single bad note from the piano they kept outside, they were flooded with every placement of where the teeth had been buried briefly after they were shown as threat. Nobody knew how many teeth hid inside a man's skull, and nobody could do the math on how many men must have been rolled into the marsh, but after the terrible storm the soupy black dirt appeared to be smiling across the whole of the county. Each boot that chased a tooth back down was declared to be guilty as hell.

The Sea Naked

She wanted the desert. She wanted to shiver only at night. The fear she brought with her, to camp under so many heavenly witnesses, he fought back, baggy with the tequila she bought, he fought back wide, and not once did he strike her face. The three seconds between the bruising and the grand leak must have looked like a celebration of good bodies from so far away, must have reminded the fathers of what the sling-shot motion can do when enough explosions take place close to the heart of all sky. At least, for a little while, it must have resembled a creation tale.

The Stuff Of Legends

Wooded, the possibility of fire is always real, that descent is constant, a lesson taught as the first lesson. That doesn't mean we are afraid of the spark. It means we don't care about ashes.

The Walls Slid Back Down, Joining

She had no time to describe the lost things, but the trail was epic, so we chased, first, where she was coming from. There was the dead, and that was expected. There was the blood that seemed to be dragged by her out into the woods to be killed again, and that disregard was maybe most impressive. It takes dedication to kill the killed and do so in a public way. What we couldn't see from any great distance was that she had demolished her parent's house as well. She didn't set any fires. She took it apart piece by piece, smashing the strong bits, being gentle where she could. It looked like a puzzle violently undone. It looked bathed in her parent's remains. She must have been working on it for months.

Through The Skin Of The Lip

I want to say so exactly the wrong thing that the words must find another way to leave my body, so exactly the wrong thing that they must kill parts of me to escape through where once there was no hole to escape from. I want to say the awful things that plum and dip inside my scattered, ecstatic freedom. I don't want it to be okay. I just want to find the sharpness of my angles of descent.

We Gave Metal To Butterflies

Beauty to gleam with the awful additions of violence, we can turn almost any animal into a threat. So, we are the biggest threat? No. Every animal waits for our additions. They were beautiful before, but now they have the sharp edges, the right trajectory, the access to our throats. Maybe nothing, an absolute nothing, should have been the plan.

We Take More Photographs Of The Dead Boy

There is a kingdom in the tightened jaw of the drowned boy. Let's keep our distance from it. Let's take more pictures of his youth, and grape to wind the signature of his passing. Other than the directness of vengeance, I feel only shame for never searching the body for a soul.

The Gym Shoe Dead

This collection of well toned or well intentioned, the guilty, they pile up like rocks by the side of the road. They are mourned by tightened guts and people that hate them. I like drunks. I liked it when I was a drunk. Drunks die squishy, finally on the fire, willing to be scenery and god dammit willing to be scenery. I go through a pair of gym shoes every six months now, but I wear that tread in my basement. No fucker in a pick-up is going to lose his breakfast burrito all over my ecstatic, fumbling lurch away from the bottles.

A Flowering Almond

Inventive as hell, the marvel is how forces can build when coupled with the right chemical. We know murder is intimate, but the continuum is cemented by the nut's fragmenting inside the progression of a station that was left by the guilty miles ago. Catch the bloom before his weight breaks through the glass door of his unsuccessful escape from the allergic reaction.

The Facts Persisted

Slender, crooked, I can hardly understand what rich flesh does without stars, but the scars always seem to rip free during daytime. The premise of blood is a color. The premise of the fault line is a color. The model and mathematics of the rest is done without light.

The High School Baseball Coach Gets Exactly What He Wanted

All fire and no smoke, he knew that if even though she was sixteen, she could lead him back to the ecstatic nature of his youth. Seven years ago he had been in college, had worn his own jersey to the parties, and his frame had proven ample enough for liberal arts victories and the liberal arts carnival that followed, and when he had asked the woman that stayed the longest to marry him, she had felt blessed by that. He was tired now. She was pregnant and he was tired, and the girl squirming over his penis with her hip-length red hair was neither of those things. He saw only the past as he neared a climax that would never come, because if he had even peeked a little at the future he would know what would happen when he up-righted his car seat. He saw the slight aging. He saw the pronounced belly. He never saw the steak knife she held in each hand. Not one of them screamed.

The Cage Is Unwound By The Poetry Of Death

Poetry is the same as collecting all of the deaths in a single county, and painting every thousandth body neon green, something to arbitrarily highlight the special moment where an exact decision was made in the chaos of the flood. On the occasion that flood brings you a painted body, know that I had everything to do with it, but almost nothing to do with what stopped the first force of being. There is only one force of being. I have no names for it. I have many names for the cowards that stick their hands in the river before the slight tide can deliver.

Somewhere Else You Will Have To Die

Let's dare the assumption of breath to be truth long enough to frame us in the context of the bold. It will look quite natural when the tree root places a deep knob against your throat. It will look like victory for the natural. The forest will trophy you for a long time before it ever puts you to use. If you die on cement, it will be your neighbors that get to play with your bones.

Strobe-Effect

If all you ever saw was the frame after the frame you wanted to see, you would want to destroy the whole film too.

Rubber Tied

They both wanted the butterfly of the bird to hold steady in the window, but those bullets pierced more than the simple skin. Already past the body on the hard wood floor, he picked up the shattered glass slowly, admiring the feathers that still floated in the air. The possibility for great beauty still remained, but it would take a terrific deal of effort to move past the visual of his gloves wrapped around the headless being he so admired. He wondered if birds carried names with them. He wondered if this bird had ever killed another bird, did it say the name of the soon to be no more? Why had he said her name before he shot straight through her snap shirt? He kept four feathers.

So Far From Lunar Air

True to the directionless pull of the human spirit, she wore the parasol as an article of clothing, and on the sunny days her breasts would burn with delight. Always misaligned, chest-to-chest with the properly clothed, the scatterings felt she might be more beast than burden, and that welcoming thought led them to create an altar for her. She killed seven of them before she ever found weakness.

Sand Overspread

We have done too much with the fossils of the past, taken them to frame them, leaving gaps on the path towards an unmoving ground. It was never supposed to be seamless, it was to be constantly shifting, and if enough granules are snared as jewels of the question, then the openness pierces our frailty. This will become an adventure story until the ashes of enough people rise to balance our footsteps. The sacrifice will be terrible to repeat.

Secret Thing

Early chant, fire and the white stem left by fire, the whole of the thing reclines so much that it would take the beast of the celestial to accommodate it. That turning has us transfixed on a picture that was never bigger than the first words and the first fire.

Skyless

If the deluge rises from the un-sifted gifts of the land, not all of us will survive that washing. Moved to be love and the absence of such, we need the dichotomy so we know then to prepare ourselves to be rinsed of the in-between. We are the in-between. When we leave the world will snap shut.

Some Folks Inherit

No matter the reasoning, the gestures of withholding can blind the recipient of all patience, and with a real quench coming down the mountain, it must seem easy to just cut down the remaining lengths of the person. The money is different, better than the freedom? If it takes all of a person to keep something away from you, what makes you think it will be easy to hold what you have coming.

It Was A Question Of Ownership

Even with an intimacy granted, wished for, desired, she had never wanted to be held nor hinted at belonging to him. The first needle was for his hand that never left her ass. The second needle was for him calling her ten times a night when she went out and he stayed at home. The third needle was for making an enemy out of her own bed. The fourth needle was for his claim that only he would love her. The fifth needle was for ripping up her favorite sweater. The sixth needle was for ripping up her favorite picture of her wearing her favorite sweater. All of the needles were bought, paid for with his credit card, because that motherfucker became so heavy that it took his blood leaving the scene for her to feel even the smallest touch of freedom.

Present And Turned Around

The bullet only elaborates the barbaric cut of the pointing, and the shout to turn isn't to avoid the cowardice of shooting a man in his back, it's to collect the facial scenes, all five of them, before the motherfucker dies.

Just A Twirling

In the middle of a motel story, the bodies are already leaking into the parking lot, though none of them appear to be damaged enough to bend in the wind, the angels with their boot heels wedged into the metal grills of the Cadillac appear to be the bad blood running the show. There are dogs barking from half of the rooms. There are no birds in sight. There is only one liquor store. It is only one block away. The empty pool will get filled one fucking way or another.

Leaning Into The Wind Doesn't Make You Part Of The Wind

The surrender is cliff only. A bunch of us poor bastards are still convinced we can fly. We never could discard each other.

Lilac Horses

Appointed to hesitate, we have pushed our animals to threaten the unsteady lines of the land once too often. Once, on a hillside in Texas, I asked the manager of a gas station why there were so many lovely, purple flowers growing a dozen or so yards behind the restroom outliers. He said they used to bury horses there, when they were allowed to do such things. He said, his grandmother always told him that horseflesh gave special gifts to the flora. I told him I thought it was weird that she believed that. It feels monstrous, I said. No shit, he responded, and with that one of us decided to keep the other's change.

An Argument Erupts Over The Naming Of Flowers

There were two women, one of them old, one of them young, and together they grew the most beautiful flowers in the whole of Know County. They lived in the dirt, shared the dirt with each other, and saved the best of it for their floral children. It was a quiet, long love. One day, instead of singing, the older woman rattled off all of the names she had given to each of the flowers. They were named after her dead husband, her children that had moved far away, her grandchildren that rarely visited, and her brother and sisters she had lost track of decades ago. Without knowing she was renaming the flowers the girl had already blessed with personal monikers, she managed to trample the spirit of the garden, and maybe that would have been fine, but the girl had arrived soon after to burn every root she had named after her boyfriend. All anyone saw was the fire growing taller than the fence line. After that there were only accusations. All of the names had been used up.

She Made It No Further Than Nebraska

Skittered to the boat dock, incredibly far from home, as low as America allows our kind to live, she had bagged the ram back home, but never examined her best friend for the scars he tended to leave on the body. Without a single gnaw on her flesh, her best friend allowed the body to find its own way through the reeds, tipped her to tag her with death, and with her pants around her ankles and no knowledge of a good thrash, she sank with casual ceremony. She had said she needed to pee. She had said it was an emergency. She was right.

In Some Towns There Is Only One Public Official And One Sex Worker

They canceled the crossing countdown for the one blind resident, that bird sound only pisses off the real birds of the town, which really is just a state route that barely winds through, enough through that the cars refuse to acknowledge the dip in speed. No matter, they all see the sex worker sitting on the picnic table outside the cold beer drive through, and since she wears only colors that clash with the blue polar bear on the car side of the building, everyone knows that quickly their world could improve with such a rainbow before them. Not a mayor, not a police officer, the township representative, once Columbia Gas management, knows that only one of them should be perched outside on that table getting drunk, but if all two hundred and twenty seven guns were trained on one target, it would be his spilling they might desire most.

It's Awful How Romantic This Is

She gave him a love that was all veer and no correction. It lasted exactly as long as it was supposed to. It lasted forever. Forever is not so long among those people who remove the shrouds from their mouths and welcome the whole of a person as a gift. She gave him one gift after another, her gifts were all poisons, beautifully bottled, as if she knew an apothecary who claimed to be a healer and finisher of all lies.

It Can't Be Reached And It Won't Go Away

There is some evidence that the way our atoms work we don't so much take things to hold them, but are constantly pushing them away from us. Gravity is the angel. Anger is the broken ocean, always spilled, never retreating. If we actually wanted to allow our bodies to be completed, it wouldn't matter, because it doesn't work like that. When we wish to take the throat of another and offer it to the moon, the moon is willing to accept, but that's not how it works either.

Kicking Horses

The first wronging is the disturbance of the world. The second is the removal of joy. Everything that happens after that is a horrid play under compromised settings. If you wait for the local animals to alert this to you, then you are already in the middle of being slain.

I Can Tell By the Way You Talk

Gwendolyn said the sun came out to show what the storm had done. You ain't, she said.

The Woman Finds Her Ex-Lover In An Alley In Philadelphia

He was never alone, even when he was with her he found other ways to be un-alone as well, so when he stumbled past her, drunk on himself and most of the bars in South Philly, she whirled around with every intention of giving him peace, giving him a chance to be alone, and yet un-alone. He would get used to the cold hands, and as long as he didn't turn around in the next five seconds, she could scream help, she could stuff her purse into the heart of his jacket, and allow it to drown in the echoes of her most primal of wishes. This sober thought was calming to her, and she could feel her own strength grip the freedom that came from her own steel loneliness. This must be what an eagle feels like before a dive into the river, she thought.

Cut the Meat

She could have been alone in the sky, but she was born thigh-deep in the mud and that left her mad with the certainty that she would be cut down by the ground bare eagerness of a man that knew how to parcel a woman. Any man that slowed down in front of her, asked her a question, demanded an answer, he would be buried without his intentions, and would never be able to rise again. She didn't care for answers. She just cared about never finding anything to compare herself to.

A Creamy Chiffon Dress

It must have looked like an angel in finishing flight, her arms braced, pressured, intent and unaware of what her gown was doing in the wind. She looked like there might be a cliff beneath her. The rocks his living person found made it seem as if there had always been a cliff beneath her, and it had just taken her arms wrapped around his cheating neck to remove the floor. The questions of trust and decisiveness can always be distracted by the right woman in the right cloth.

Brazen Lake Superior

Let somebody else worry about the un-buried flesh. Spring will come and the water will become much more accepting of such sins. Until then, the not-so-thin defiance of Lake Superior will keep the murders propped like puppets, unwilling to mount the slightest tide of revival. That water always makes a point, belabors the point, becomes obnoxious with the point.

Cockleshells

Sheltered, the sea still flees, still finds us to return us to the turning silt. If we are picked up then we are already dead. If we live forever in seclusion then we were never really alive. We must, at our best, take on the ocean.

Before She Put The Photograph To Her Chest She Flipped The Face Away From Her Flesh

A mother in the mirror still needs to see the faces of her children. He had been an awful man, but as a boy he was still her flowering weed, something she could color as a flower from some distance. He murdered those people. She thought about that. She wished he hadn't done it, though she couldn't simply wish him away from her heart. She held this picture of her boy gently at first, but before she turned off the lights of the bathroom, she felt her hand tighten over the picture of his developing face.

The Black Belly Star Dances Too

It was the first star that decided not enough people were dying with a soundtrack. This is why we are, now, running out room to the layer our dust. Soon, we might have whole mountains made out of people that loved Bob Dylan too much to hear their front door lock jimmy open.

Blank Light

Sometimes the void is influentially bright. Sometimes there is no color, no desire, no imagery of self or the exploration of self. There are moments simply too vacant for human beings to handle. We tend to fill those moments one way or another. We tend to spill ourselves all over those moments. The cowards are shamed into spilling others. The cowards paint the whole world with others.

An Impression

It was a superb death, to vanish beneath the frozen lake, to find the one weakness in miles of strength.

An Imperfect Comb

We have solved most threshing. We have no idea what to do with the almost gentle deaths, the takings, the push to perish, the finger guiding our shoulders to swing with the beginnings of violence.

A Misinterpretation of Big Love

It was a quick question, an all-sorted-out delivery, and the simple answer was the ocean. It felt like the ocean, at first water, and at second all too much water. One thimble is, could be the rest of the world if your eyes and stomach can handle a good hunger. Some men use both hands to cradle and consume their love. They never last too long. They always become shells, their fat leaking past the beach, their bone un-tender in the mouths of fish.

A Generous Sample Of Enlightenment

He killed three men to prove he was the lightning and they were simply an invention of their times.

When the Swimmer Drowns

Healthy until the holes were pushed through him, took circular pieces of his flesh and exploded them into a star shape for the fish to explore, he was a boat they said, he could spend all day in the water. He was a boat they said, he could be found in water. He was a boat they said, with enough separation between his ribs the water could reach in and take him down deep enough to be home forever. The river he swam crossed several county lines quickly, snaked through the triangle that led through into Knox, and all those trees just kept providing cover for a rifle. Anyone could have fired those shots. He was a boat, they said. Everybody also said he was an asshole and a liar.

The Girl Was A Raspberry

Killing a mile of steam at a time, the fog pouring like the best lies that can trace the valley with a plastic bag tenderness, and that girl, I tell you, she was a raspberry, she said she had real skin, but the world around her could only be swallowed, never chewed without leaving moments of terror around the mouths of all the boys she called to. I know her fatalities talked more without the days counting them, and I also know her tight intentions could be like seeds beginning to grow underneath a molar. No man had straight teeth after he met her. Part of that was because they were valley people. Part of that was that she wouldn't lay down with any of them without a large tree branch within her thick arm's reach.

Caribou

Rush the darkness. Bend your head down. Allow your crown to plunge through the urgency. If there really was a person there, will it ever matter to you? It should, but then again it isn't always about should. There are whole nations that have been dug up. They were faithful, intent on good, and it took only one ambition to render their poignancy moot. Sometimes you are in a forest of people. Sometimes those people carry no seed.

Acknowledgements

Botticelli Magazine – Unfinished Murder Ballad: In Some Towns There Is Only One Public Official and One Prostitute; Unfinished Murder Ballad: When the Swimmer Drowns; Unfinished Murder Ballad: The Woman Finds Her Ex-Lover in An Alley in Philadelphia

Dalhousie Review – Unfinished Murder Ballad: The Only Dedicated Cowboy in Columbus, Ohio Objects to the Price of His Black Coffee

Fourteen Hills – Unfinished Murder Ballad: The Girl Was A Raspberry

Helix Literary Review – Unfinished Murder Ballad: Unfinished Murder Ballad: The Inventor of Small Things Ends His Denial

Jet Fuel Review – Unfinished Murder Ballad: The Sea Naked

The Round – Unfinished Murder Ballad: Secret Thing

Screaming Sheep – Unfinished Murder Ballad: It Can't Be Reached and It Won't Go Away

Unbroken – Unfinished Murder Ballad: Blank Light; Unfinished Murder Ballad: Caibou

Writer's Bloc – Unfinished Murder Ballad: An Argument Erupts Over the Naming of Flowers; Unfinished Murder Ballad: It Was A Question of Ownership

Zaira – Unfinished Murder Ballad: The Walls Slid Back Down

www.ingramcontent.com/pod-product-compliance
Lightning Source LLC
Chambersburg PA
CBHW030332230426
43661CB00032B/1379/J